Sight Words

Level A

55 words

you need to know
to be a successful reader

Written by Shannon Keeley • Illustrated by Janee Trasler

Flash Kids

ISBN-13: 978-1-4114-0490-8
ISBN-10: 1-4114-0490-4

For more information please visit *www.flashkidsbooks.com*
Please submit changes or report errors to *www.flashkidsbooks.com/errors*

Printed and bound in China

Spark Publishing
120 Fifth Avenue
New York, NY 10011

Dear Parent,

Every time your child reads a text, 50–75% of the words he or she encounters are from the Dolch Sight Word List. The Dolch Sight Word List is a core group of 220 common words that are repeated frequently in reading material. Children need extra practice learning these words, many of which can't be represented by simple pictures. Often, these sight words do not follow regular spelling rules and cannot be "sounded out." So, learning to immediately recognize these words "at sight" is a critical skill for fluent reading. This is the first book in a series that covers all 220 Dolch sight words. The 55 words covered in this book are listed below. The activities in this book offer lots of practice with tracing and writing, as well as fun word puzzles and games. Your child can color the pictures, laugh at the funny characters, and enjoy learning about sight words.

The sight words included in this book are:

a	did	in	on	three
all	down	is	one	to
am	find	it	play	two
and	for	like	ran	up
away	funny	little	red	was
be	go	look	run	we
big	good	make	said	what
blue	he	me	see	where
but	help	my	so	yellow
can	here	no	that	yes
come	I	not	the	you

Say the word a aloud as you trace it.

a

Now practice writing the word once on each line.

I see  bird.

Careful Crossing

Show how the bunny crosses the stream. Cross out each rock that does not have the word a inside.

 **Say the word go aloud as you trace it.**

_____

Now practice writing the word once on each line.

_____

. . . .

_____

_____

. . . .

_____

. . . .

_____

_____

. . . .

_____

Let's _____ in the house.

Stay on Track

The word **go** is hidden two times on each track.
Find the words and circle them.

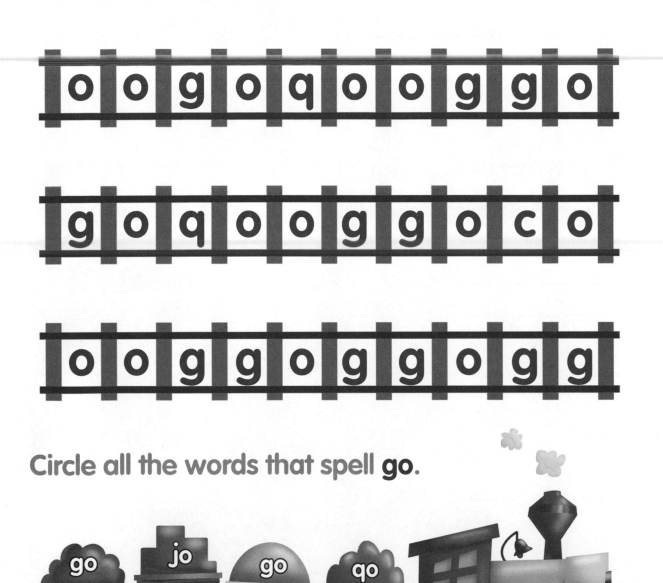

o o g o q o o g g o

g o q o o g g o c o

o o g g o g g o g g

Circle all the words that spell **go**.

go   jo   go   qo

goo   go   gow   go

up

say the word up aloud as you trace it.

_____

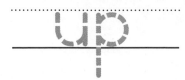

Now practice writing the word once on each line.

_____

....

_____

....

_____

....

_____

....

_____

My cat is _____ in the tree!

Lucky Letters

Write **up** on the line under each lucky clover that makes the word **up**.

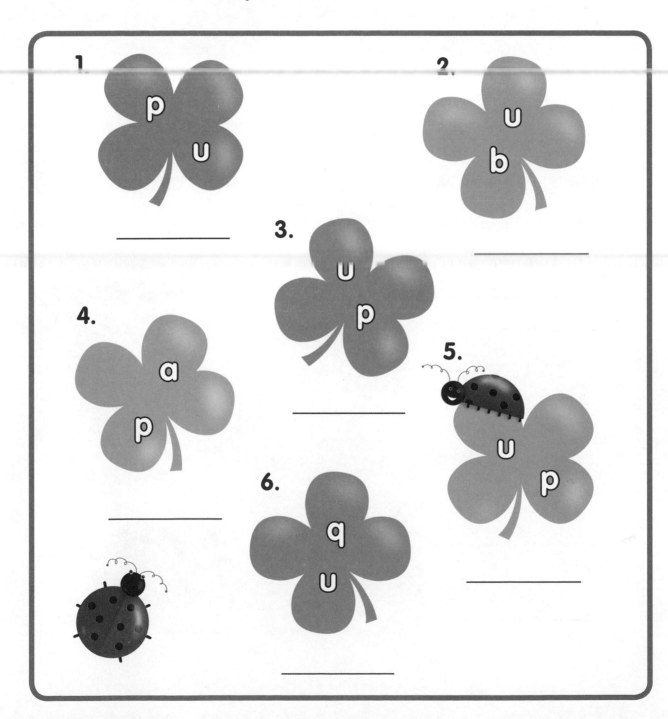

**you** Say the word you aloud as you trace it.

you

Now practice writing the word once on each line.

Do _____ like ice cream?

Dot-to-Dot

Draw lines to connect the letters y-o-u and complete the picture.

 **for**

say the word **for** aloud as you trace it.

for

Now practice writing the word once on each line.

This is _____ you.

Hide and Seek

Some of the words in the treetop have **for** hidden inside. Find the words and write them on the lines below. Circle the letters **f-o-r** in each word.

fork

foot

frog   four

from

form

fort

forget

_____   _____

_____

Review: Word Search

Find each word in the word search.

a   go   up   you   for

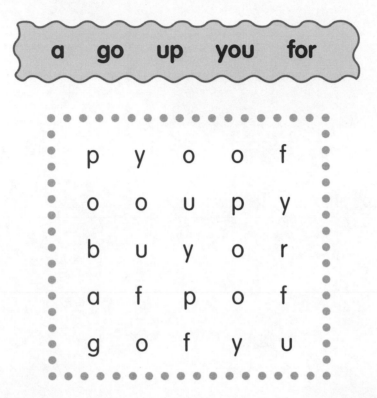

p	y	o	o	f
o	o	u	p	y
b	u	y	o	r
a	f	p	o	f
g	o	f	y	u

Color the box that has all five review words spelled correctly.

1.	2.	3.	4.	5.
a	a	a	a	e
goe	go	go	go	go
up	up	op	up	ub
you	you	you	yuo	you
far	for	for	fur	for

Review: Wormy Words

Read each sentence. Every time you see one of the review words, circle it. Then count how many circled words are in each sentence.

1. Dad got a dog for me. ◯

2. Will you go up the hill? ◯

3. Let's go get a snack. ◯

4. Can you go for a hike? ◯

5. It's time to go home. ◯

The worm with the most words wins the race! Which worm is the winner? _____

Write your own sentence. Use as many of the review words as you can.

_____

 **say the word the aloud as you trace it.**

Now practice writing the word once on each line.

Open _____ book.

Tic-Tac-Toe

Circle the row that spells the word **the**.

t	e	t
h	h	e
t	e	e

Circle the row that has the word **the** three times.

the	tbe	the
hte	teh	the
thh	the	the

Say the word is aloud as you trace it.

is

Now practice writing the word once on each line.

This _____ my dog.

Lost and Found

The word is is hidden once in each line. Find the word and circle the letters.

s	j	i	z	i	s
1	2	3	4	5	6

j	s	i	s	i	z
1	2	3	4	5	6

i	s	s	i	z	j
1	2	3	4	5	6

To complete the message, look at the number below each circled letter. Find the matching number in the message below and write the letter on the line.

H___ ___ hat ___ ___ ___n
  1   2   3   4   5

the ___ ink.
     6

away

Say the word away aloud as you trace it.

_____

.......away.......

Now practice writing the word once on each line.

_____

....

_____

_____

....

_____

_____

....

_____

Let's put _____ the toys.

Linking Letters

Draw a line to link the letters that make the word **away**.

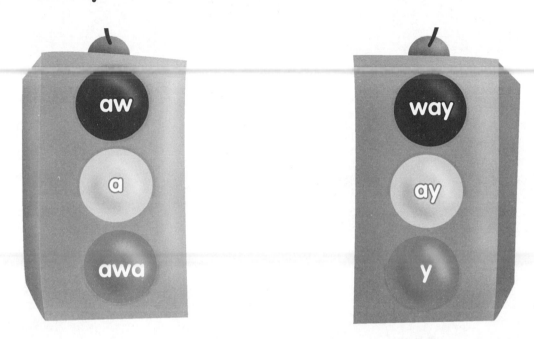

Write the missing letters to make the word **away**.

a___ a___

___ ___ay

a___ ___ y

___ w ___ y

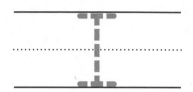 say the word **I** aloud as you trace it.

Now practice writing the word once on each line.

_____ am at the top.

Follow the Line

Circle the word I in each sentence. Then draw a line to connect the circled words, and see which letters you pass through. Write the letters below to answer the riddle.

1. I like ice cream.

    a   o   c   b   n

2. Dad and I went to get ice cream.

    w   e   g   n   r

3. "It's a big scoop," I said.

    c   a   b   q   m

4. It was much more than I could eat.

    d   a   p   e   o

5. So I shared it with my dad.

What did the cone say to the ice cream?

Dessert is ____ ____ ____ ____ !

 **say the word and aloud as you trace it.**

Now practice writing the word once on each line.

I put on my socks _____ shoes.

Rhyme Time

Circle the pictures that rhyme with **and**. Underline the letters a-n-d in each word.

sand

hang

stand

sad

pan

hand

land

ant

Review: Word Search

Find each word in the word search.

the   is   I   away   and

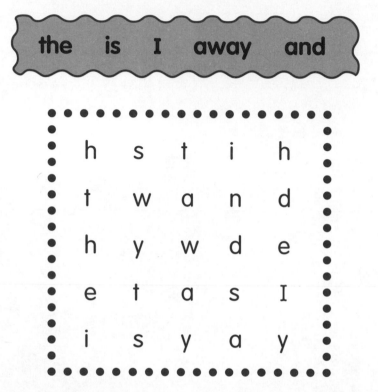

```
h   s   t   i   h
t   w   a   n   d
h   y   w   d   e
e   t   a   s   I
i   s   y   a   y
```

Color the box that has all five review words spelled correctly.

1.	2.	3.	4.	5.
the	thu	the	the	the
iz	is	is	is	si
away	away	awhy	away	awye
I	I	i	I	I
anb	ahd	and	and	and

Review: Story Surprise

Write the correct word from the word box to complete each sentence in the story.

the   I   is   away   and

My dog's name ___ ___ Roofus.
           1

I took him to ___ ___ ___ beach.

Roofus played ___ ___ ___ I swam.
            2   3   4

Then, ___ couldn't find him!

Did he run ___ ___ ___ ___?

For each number in the story sentences, find the matching number below. Write the letter on the line to find out what happened!

Where was Roofus?
Roofus was under the ___ ___ ___ ___.
                     1   2   3   4

 **big**

Say the word big aloud as you trace it.

big

Now practice writing the word once on each line.

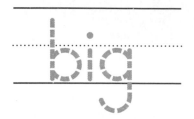

This hat is _____.

Careful Crossing

Show how the frog crosses the pond. Cross out each lily pad that does not have the word big inside.

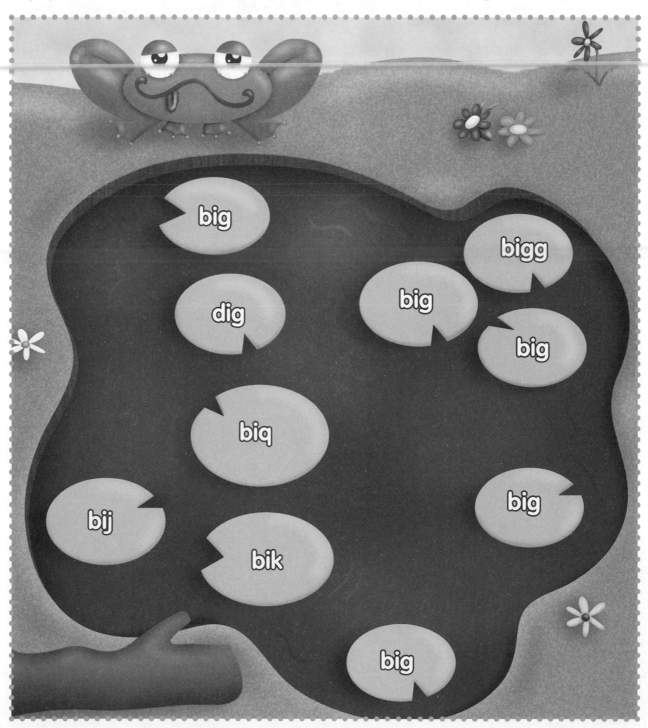

 **to**

Say the word to aloud as you trace it.

Now practice writing the word once on each line.

Let's go _____ the park.

Stay on Track

The word **to** is hidden two times on each track. Find the words and circle them.

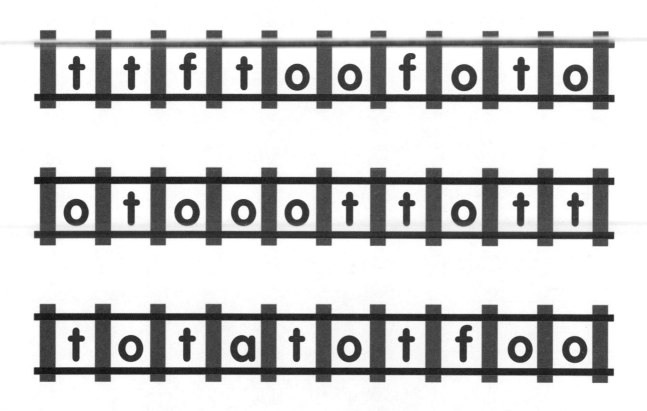

```
t  t  f  t  o  o  f  o  t  o
o  t  o  o  o  t  t  o  t  t
t  o  t  a  t  o  t  f  o  o
```

Circle all the words that spell **to**.

too   ot   to   tto
to   to   ttoo to

 **look**

say the word look aloud as you trace it.

look

Now practice writing the word once on each line.

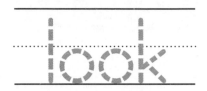

Hey, _____ at me go!

Lucky Letters

Write **look** on the line under each lucky clover that makes the word **look**.

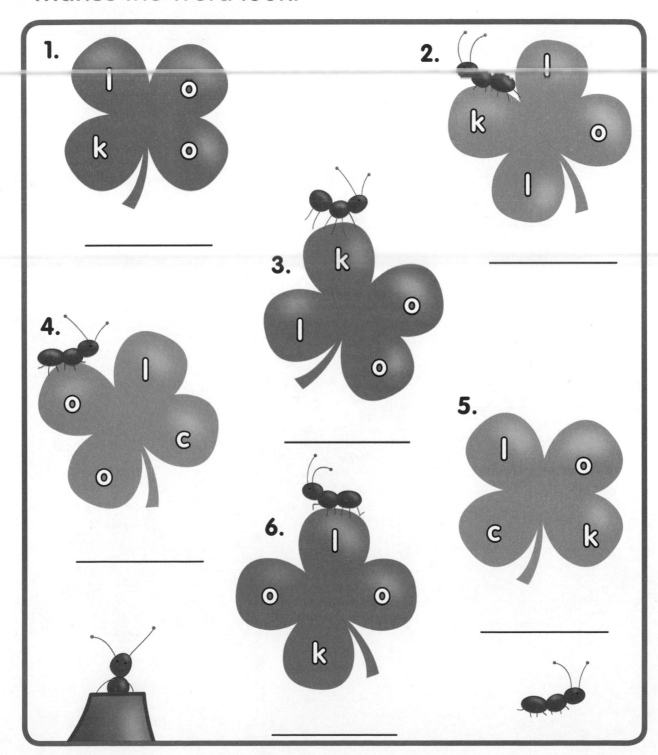

1. _____

2. _____

3. _____

4. _____

5. _____

6. _____

 **say the word run aloud as you trace it.**

······run

Now practice writing the word once on each line.

I can _____ up the hill.

Dot-to-Dot

Draw lines to connect the letters r-u-n and complete the picture.

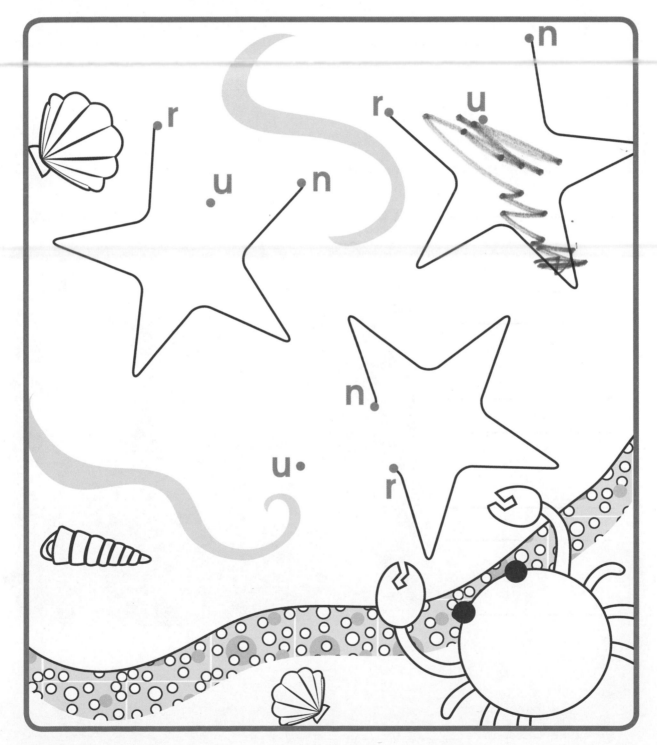

Say the word see aloud as you trace it.

see

Now practice writing the word once on each line.

I can _____ the moon.

Hide and Seek

Some of the words in the treetop have **see** hidden inside. Find the words and write them on the lines below. Circle the letters **s-e-e** in each word.

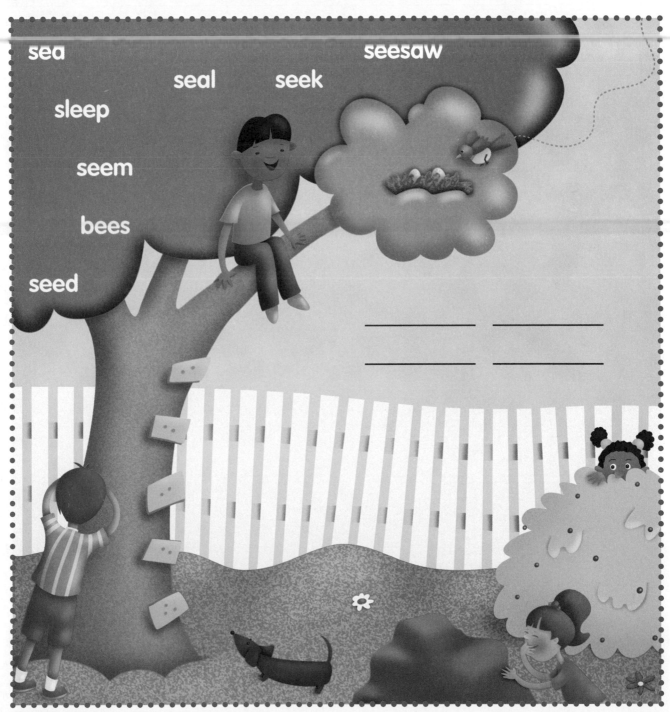

sea

seesaw

seal   seek

sleep

seem

bees

seed

_____ _____

_____ _____

Review: Word Search

Find each word in the word search.

big   to   look   run   see

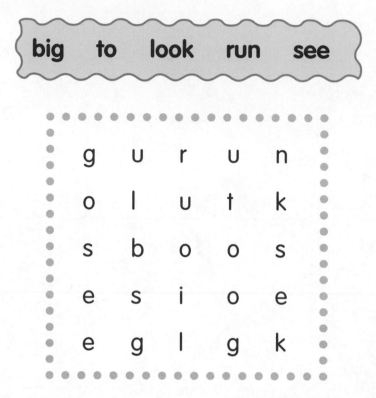

g	u	r	u	n
o	l	u	t	k
s	b	o	o	s
e	s	i	o	e
e	g	l	g	k

Color the box that has all five review words spelled correctly.

1.	2.	3.	4.	5.
big	big	bip	big	big
look	look	look	loock	look
to	ta	to	to	ot
run	ron	ruh	run	run
see	see	see	se	see

Review: Wormy Words

Read each sentence. Every time you see one of the review words, circle it. Then count how many circled words are in each sentence.

1. See me run up the big hill! ◯

2. Let's look at the new book. ◯

3. Can you run to the park? ◯

4. Let's run to see Dad. ◯

5. Look at the big dog run to me. ◯

The worm with the most words wins the race! Which worm is the winner? _____

Write your own sentence. Use as many of the review words as you can.

_____

not say the word **not** aloud as you trace it.

_____

not

Now practice writing the word once on each line.

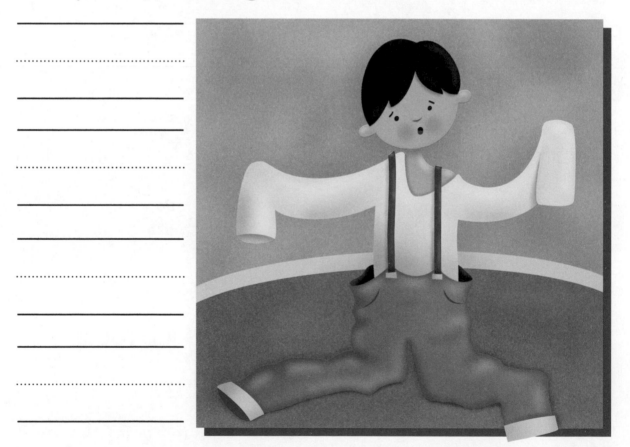

This does _____ fit.

Tic-Tac-Toe

Circle the row that spells the word **not**.

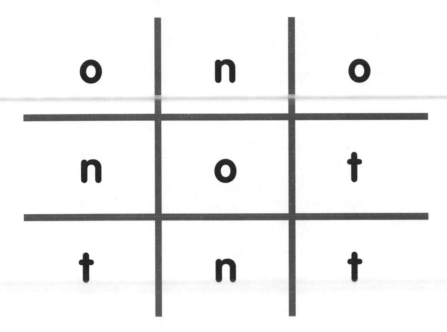

o	n	o
n	o	t
t	n	t

Circle the row that has the word **not** three times.

not	nat	not
not	nof	not
hot	not	not

 **say the word me aloud as you trace it.**

me

Now practice writing the word once on each line.

This one is for _____.

Lost and Found

The word me is hidden once in each line. Find the word and circle the letters.

e	m	m	e	e	m
1	2	3	4	5	6

e	m	n	e	m	e
1	2	3	4	5	6

m	e	e	m	m	i
1	2	3	4	5	6

To complete the message, look at the number below each circled letter. Find the matching number in the message below and write the letter on the line.

Sa___'s n___w ___ ___dal is under
    1   2   3   4

the ___ ___s s.
       5   6

here

say the word here aloud as you trace it.

here

Now practice writing the word once on each line.

Please put it _____.

Linking Letters

Draw a line to link the letters that make the word **here**.

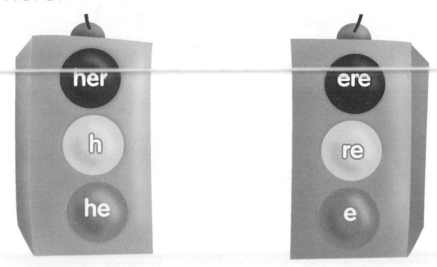

Write the missing letters to make the word **here**.

 **say the word can aloud as you trace it.**

_____

Now practice writing the word once on each line.

_____
....
_____
_____
....
_____
_____
....
_____
....
_____

I _____ go fast.

Follow the Line

Circle the word **can** in each sentence. Then draw a line to connect the circled words, and see which letters you pass through. Write the letters below to answer the riddle.

1. I can help at home.

m   p   r   w   a

2. Folding clothes is one thing I can do.

o   s   d   b   a

3. I can get it done quickly.

s   n   z   k   t

4. Can you help me at home too?

d   h   p   b   c

5. I think I can!

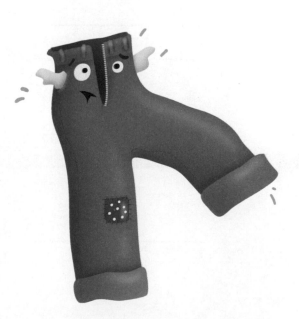

What did the old jeans say?

I'm all ____ ____ ____ ____ed up!

Say the word in aloud as you trace it.

in

Now practice writing the word once on each line.

My lunch is _____ the bag.

Rhyme Time

Circle the pictures that rhyme with in. Underline the letters i-n in each word.

chin

sign

him

fan

pin

lion

win

fin

Review: Word Search

Find each word in the word search.

not   me   here   can   in

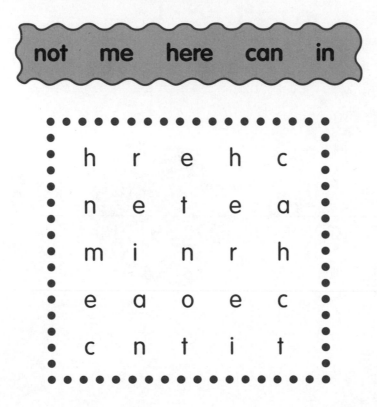

Color the box that has all five review words spelled correctly.

1.	2.	3.	4.	5.
nat	not	not	not	not
me	mee	me	me	me
nere	here	here	heer	here
can	can	cah	can	can
in	in	in	in	in

Review: Story Surprise

Write the correct word from the word box to complete each sentence in the story.

not   me   here   in   can

My brother plays hide and seek with ___ ___.

I can hide ___ ___ the kitchen.
3

"Ready or ___ ___ ___ , here I come!" he says.
46

He'll never find me in ___ ___ ___ ___.
5

___ ___ ___ you find me?
12

For each number in the story sentences, find the matching number below. Write the letter on the line to find out what happened!

Where is he?
He's hiding in the ___ ___ b ___ ___ ___ ___.
123456

**find**

say the word
find aloud as
you trace it.

find

Now practice writing the word once on each line.

Try to _____ me.

Careful Crossing

Show how the explorer goes across the hot lava. Cross out each rock that does not have the word **find** inside.

fimb

find

fim

fime

find

find

fid

find

find

fidd

 **Say the word one aloud as you trace it.**

⠄⠄⠄one

Now practice writing the word once on each line.

There is only _____ more.

Stay on Track

The word **one** is hidden two times on each track. Find the words and circle them.

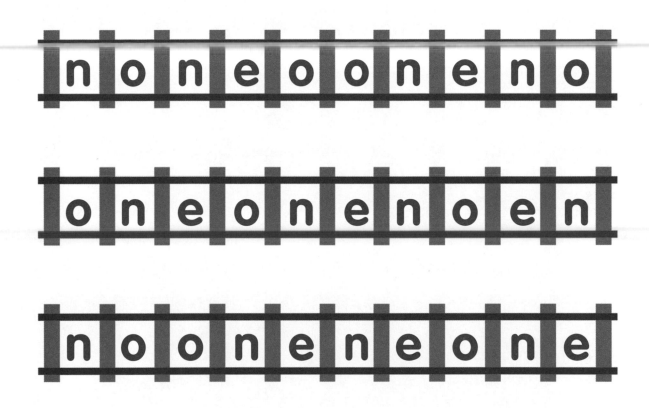

n o n e o o n e n o

o n e o n e n o e n

n o o n e n e o n e

Circle all the words that spell **one**.

on

one

onn

oee

one

one

ome

one

Say the word said aloud as you trace it.

said

Now practice writing the word once on each line.

Dad _____ to be careful.

Lucky Letters

Write said on the line under each lucky clover that makes the word said.

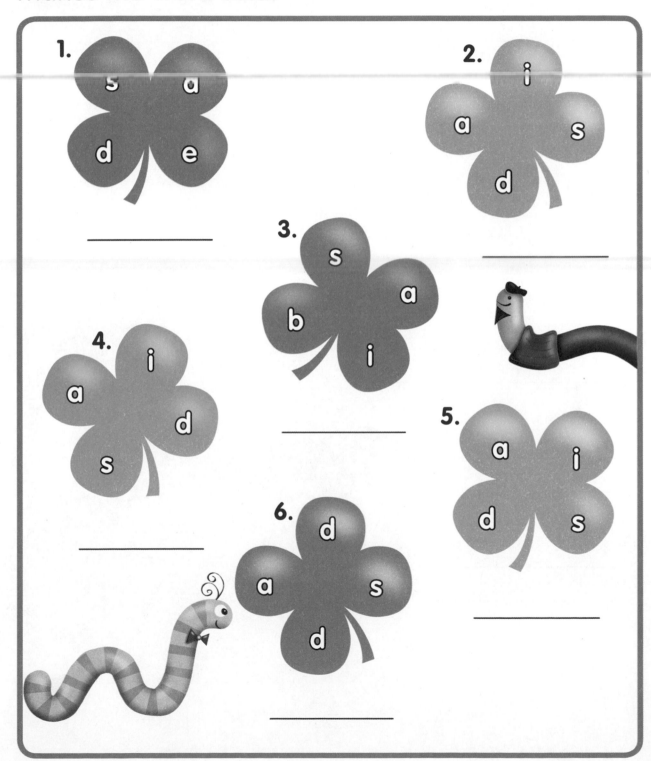

1. s a d e _____

2. i a s d _____

3. s b a i _____

4. i a d s _____

5. a i d s _____

6. d a s d _____

Say the word where aloud as you trace it.

where

Now practice writing the word once on each line.

This is _____ I live.

Dot-to-Dot

Draw lines to connect the letters w-h-e-r-e and complete the picture.

 **Say the word ran aloud as you trace it.**

ran

Now practice writing the word once on each line.

I _____ very fast!

Hide and Seek

Some of the words in the treetop have **ran** hidden inside. Find the words and write them on the lines below. Circle the letters **r-a-n** in each word.

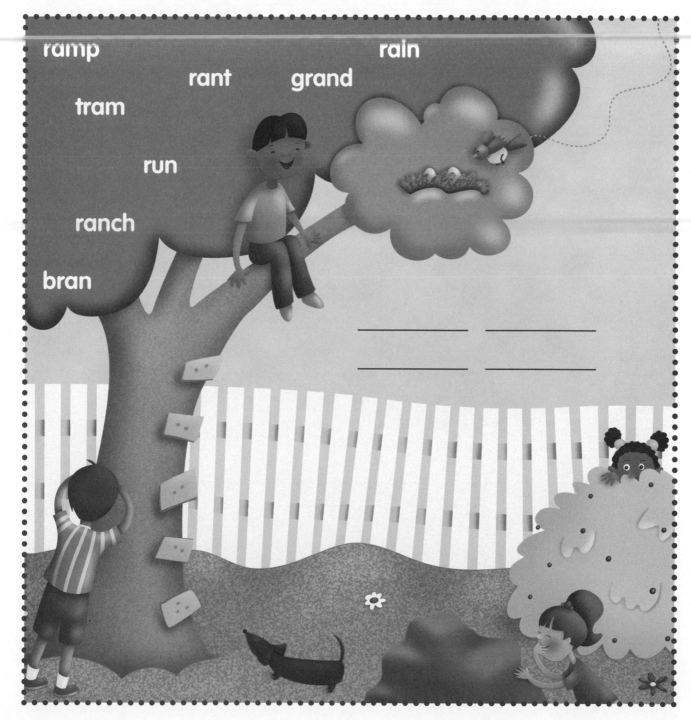

ramp

rant   grand   rain

tram

run

ranch

bran

_____ _____

_____ _____

Review: Word Search

Find each word in the word search.

find   one   said   where   ran

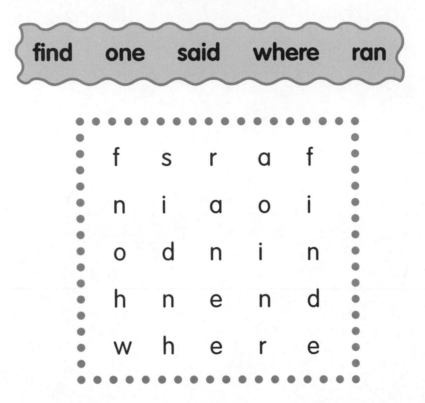

Color the box that has all five review words spelled correctly.

1.	2.	3.	4.	5.
fid	find	find	find	find
one	onn	one	one	oen
said	said	said	saib	said
where	whre	where	where	where
nan	ran	ran	ran	ran

Review: Wormy Words

Read each sentence. Every time you see one of the review words, circle it. Then count how many circled words are in each sentence.

1. I can't find where one thing is! ◯

2. Mom said where to find one. ◯

3. We ran all the way to school. ◯

4. I ran home to find my homework. ◯

5. Dad said I could have one cookie. ◯

The worm with the most words wins the race! Which worm is the winner? _____

Write your own sentence. Use as many of the review words as you can.

_____

 **say the word red aloud as you trace it.**

red

Now practice writing the word once on each line.

The fire truck is _____.

Tic-Tac-Toe

Circle the row that spells the word **red**.

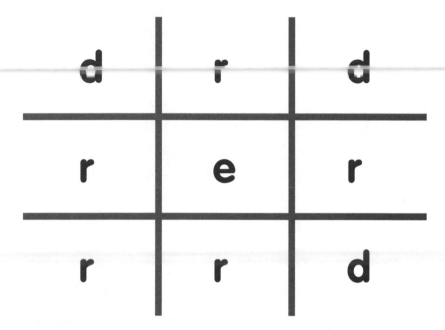

d	r	d
r	e	r
r	r	d

Circle the row that has the word **red** three times.

red	red	ned
wed	red	red
rde	red	rod

 **down** say the word down aloud as you trace it.

Now practice writing the word once on each line.

I can go _____ the slide.

Lost and Found

The word **down** is hidden once in each line. Find the word and circle the letters.

d	w	d	o	d	o	w	n
1	2	3	4	5	6	7	8

d	o	w	n	d	o	w	d
1	2	3	4	5	6	7	8

To complete the message, look at the number below each circled letter. Find the matching number in the message below and write the letter on the line.

Sam's ___ ___ g is ___ear the ___ i ___ ___ ___ ___.
    1   2   4   3   8   5   6   7

 **say the word play aloud as you trace it.**

play

Now practice writing the word once on each line.

Let's _____ ball!

Linking Letters

Draw a line to link the letters that make the word **play**.

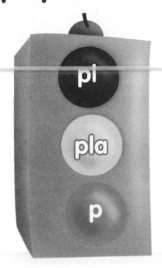 

Write the missing letters to make the word **play**.

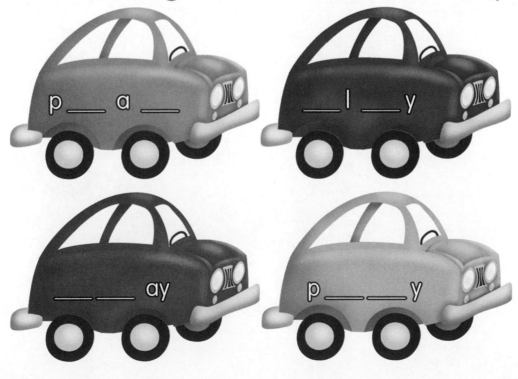

p___ a ___

___ l ___ y

___ ___ ___ ay

p ___ ___ y

 **come** say the word come aloud as you trace it.

come

Now practice writing the word once on each line.

You can _____ with me.

Follow the Line

Circle the word come in each sentence. Then draw a line to connect the circled words, and see which letters you pass through. Write the letters below to answer the riddle.

1. Everywhere I go, my dog will come along.

    n   l   b   r   w

2. "Come here," I shout.

    m   h   a   o   t

3. He will always come running.

    c   o   u   k   t

4. He barks when he wants to come with me.

    u   s   v   i   c

5. He can't come with me to school!

What type of dog always knows what time it is?

A _____ _____ _____ _____ h dog!

Say the word am aloud as you trace it.

_____

am

Now practice writing the word once on each line.

I _____ very tall.

Rhyme Time

Circle the pictures that rhyme with am. Underline the letters a-m in each word.

man

clam

slam

jam

ham

van

arm

palm

Review: Word Search

Find each word in the word search.

red   down   play   come   am

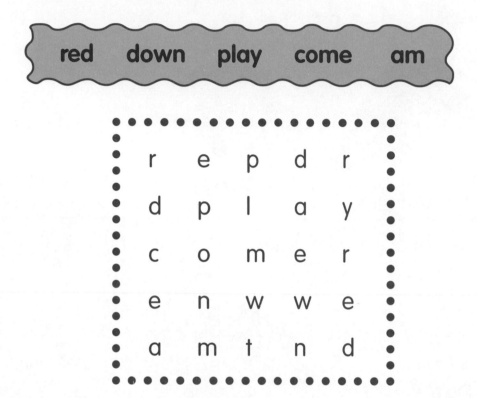

```
r  e  p  d  r
d  p  l  a  y
c  o  m  e  r
e  n  w  w  e
a  m  t  n  d
```

Color the box that has all five review words spelled correctly.

1.	2.	3.	4.	5.
red	red	reb	red	red
dovn	down	down	down	down
play	blay	play	play	plya
com	come	cume	come	come
an	ann	an	am	an

Review: Story Surprise

Write the correct word from the word box to complete each sentence in the story.

red   down   play   come   am

I asked Beth to __ __ __ __ over.
                    1

We decided to __ __ __ __ in my tree house.
              2 3 4

Beth said, "I __ __ hungry."
             5

We didn't want to get __ __ __ __ from the tree house.
                        6

What did we eat that is __ __ __ and juicy?

For each number in the story sentences, find the matching number below. Write the letter on the line to find out what happened!

What did we eat?
We ate ___ ___   ___ ___p___ ___ from the tree.
      5 6   4 2 3 1

Review: Puzzle

Look at each set of boxes. Find the word whose letters fit in the boxes.

a   I   up   to   is
big   and   can   you   away
look play said here where

1. c a n

2.

3.

4.

5.

6.

7.

8.

9.

10.

11.

12.

13.

14.

15.

Review: Riddle

Use the code to fill in the missing letters and solve the riddle.

go: s   for: r   run: A   see: p   not: l

me: p   in: s   find: a   one: r   am: o

here: e   ran: i   red: f   down: p   come: i

What do you call two banana peels?

____ ____ ____ ____ ____ ____ ____
run   see find ran for   am   red

____ ____ ____ ____ ____ ____ ____ ____
in   not come me   down here one go

my

Say the word **my** aloud as you trace it.

Now practice writing the word once on each line.

This is _____ lunch.

Careful Crossing

Show how the lizard crosses the swamp. Cross out each log that does not have the word **my** inside.

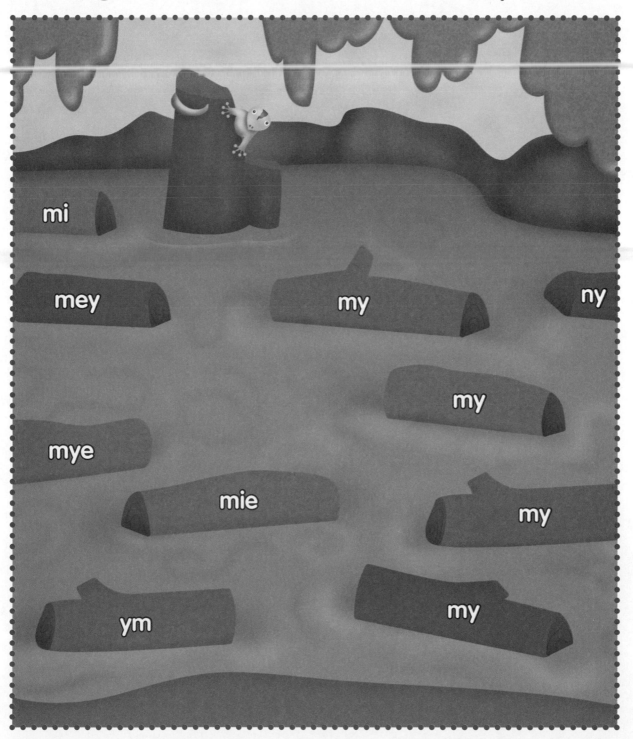

 **say the word two aloud as you trace it.**

Now practice writing the word once on each line.

I have _____ feet.

Stay on Track

The word **two** is hidden two times on each track.
Find the words and circle them.

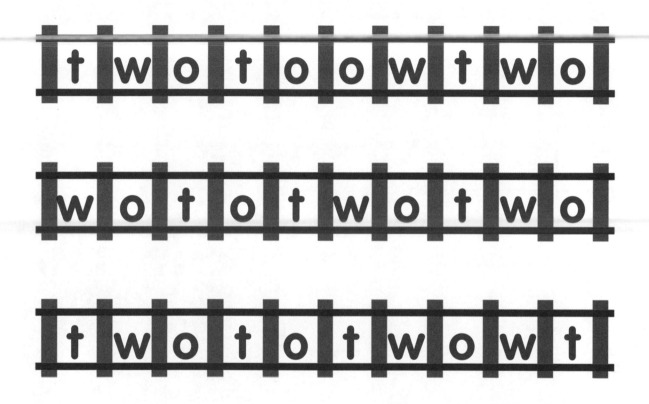

| t | w | o | t | o | o | w | t | w | o |

| w | o | t | o | t | w | o | t | w | o |

| t | w | o | t | o | t | w | o | w | t |

Circle all the words that spell **two**.

two   tow   two   twoo

two   wot   two   tuo

 **but** say the word **but**
aloud as you trace it.

but

Now practice writing the word once on each line.

My brother likes gum,
I don't.

Lucky Letters

Write **but** on the line under each lucky clover that makes the word **but**.

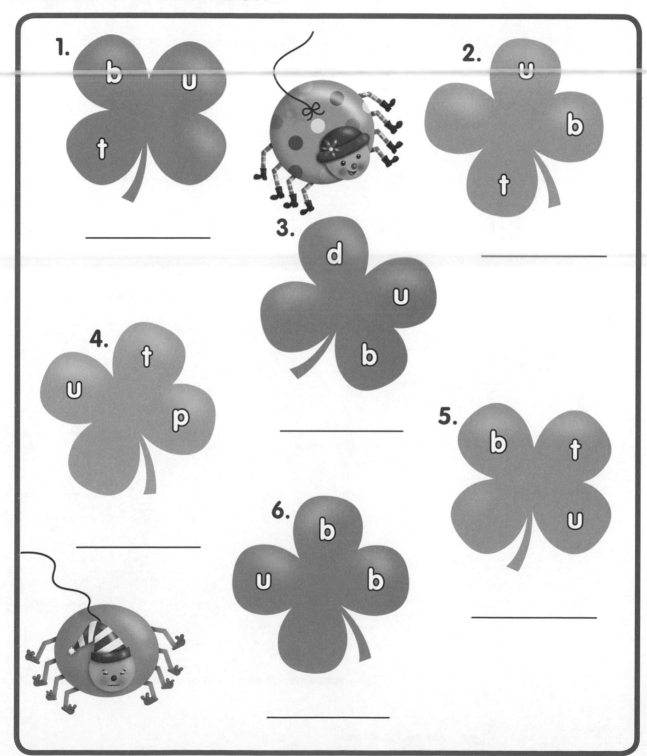

1.

_____

2.

_____

3.

_____

4.

_____

5.

_____

6.

_____

yellow

Say the word yellow aloud as you trace it.

yellow

Now practice writing the word once on each line.

The lemon is _____.

Dot-to-Dot

Draw lines to connect the letters y-e-l-l-o-w and complete the picture.

good

say the word
good aloud as
you trace it.

good

Now practice writing the word once on each line.

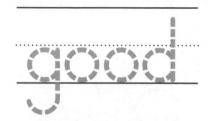

My lunch was _____.

Hide and Seek

Some of the words in the treetop have good hidden inside. Find the words and write them on the lines below. Circle the letters g-o-o-d in each word.

goodnight

goat

golfer   goodbye

goodness

goodly

gooseberry

goldfish

_____ _____

_____ _____

Review: Word Search

Find each word in the word search.

my   two   but   yellow   good

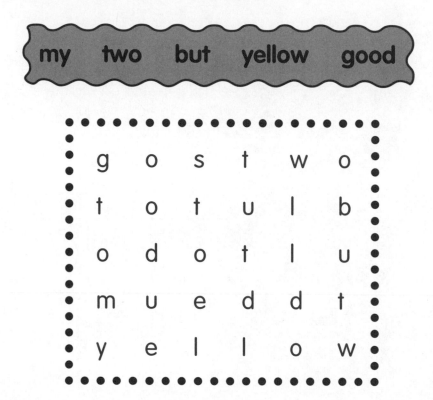

Color the box that has all five review words spelled correctly.

1.	2.	3.	4.	5.
my	my	ny	my	my
two	twu	two	two	two
but	but	but	bot	but
yellow	yellow	yellaw	yelow	yellow
good	gode	good	good	goud

Review: Story Surprise

Write the correct word from the word box to complete each sentence in the story.

my   two   but   yellow   good

There is a tree in ___ ___ backyard.
                    1

The ___ ___ ___ ___ ___ ___ lemons are ready to eat.
    2   3

We had ___ ___ ___ yellow lemons today.
       4

I went to pick them, ___ ___ ___ they were gone.

My mom used them to make something ___ ___ ___ ___ !
                                     5   6

For each number in the story sentences, find the matching number below. Write the letter on the line to find out what happened!

What did she make?

A ___lass of ___ ___ ___ ___ n a ___ e.
  5   3   2   1   4   6

 **say the word was aloud as you trace it.**

......was

Now practice writing the word once on each line.

I _____ a cat for Halloween.

Tic-Tac-Toe

Circle the row that spells the word was.

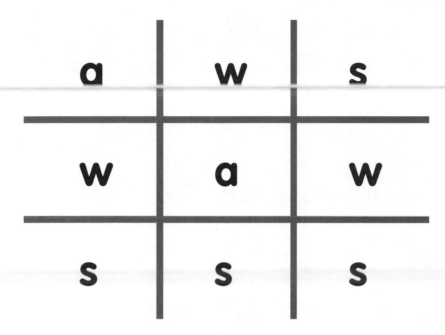

a	w	s
w	a	w
s	s	s

Circle the row that has the word was three times.

was	was	saw
mas	wsa	was
was	was	was

 **three** say the word three aloud as you trace it.

Now practice writing the word once on each line.

I have _____ boxes.

Lost and Found

The word **three** is hidden once in each line. Find the word and circle the letters.

t	h	r	e	e	t	r	e	e	h
1	2	3	4	5	6	7	8	9	10

t	h	r	e	t	t	h	r	e	e
1	2	3	4	5	6	7	8	9	10

To complete the message, look at the number below each circled letter. Find the matching number in the message below and write the letter on the line.

Sam's s___ o___s a___ ___ in ___ ___e ___ ___ ___ ___.
       2   4   3 5   6 7   1 8 9 10

 **little**

say the word little aloud as you trace it.

little

Now practice writing the word once on each line.

The baby is _____.

Linking Letters

Draw a line to link the letters that make the word **little**.

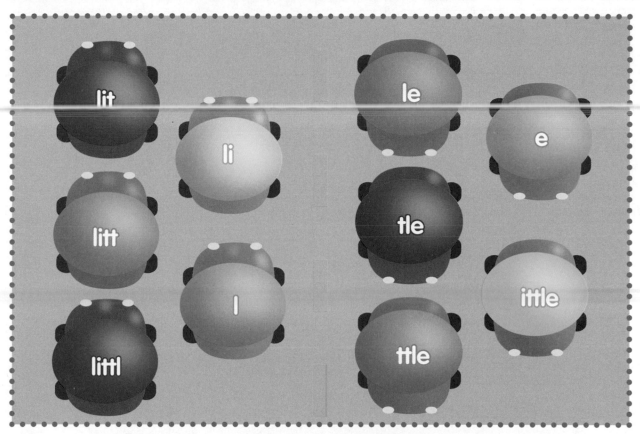

Write the missing letters to make the word **little**.

 **help** *say the word* **help** *aloud as you trace it.*

Now practice writing the word once on each line.

I can _____ you.

Follow the Line

Circle the word **help** in each sentence. Then draw a line to connect the circled words, and see which letters you pass through. Write the letters below to answer the riddle.

1. I always help my mom.

d   g   n   u   b

2. Sometimes she asks me to help make dinner.

v   s   i   y   a

3. I like to help her in the kitchen.

t   i   l   q   m

4. I can help my mom cook the food.

u   o   h   x   a

5. When dinner is ready, I can help eat it all up!

Why did the kids eat dinner on a seesaw?

To have a well- ___ ___ ___ ___ nced meal!

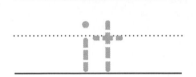 **say the word it aloud as you trace it.**

it

Now practice writing the word once on each line.

I made _____ for you.

Rhyme Time

Circle the pictures that rhyme with **it**. Underline the letters **i-t** in each word.

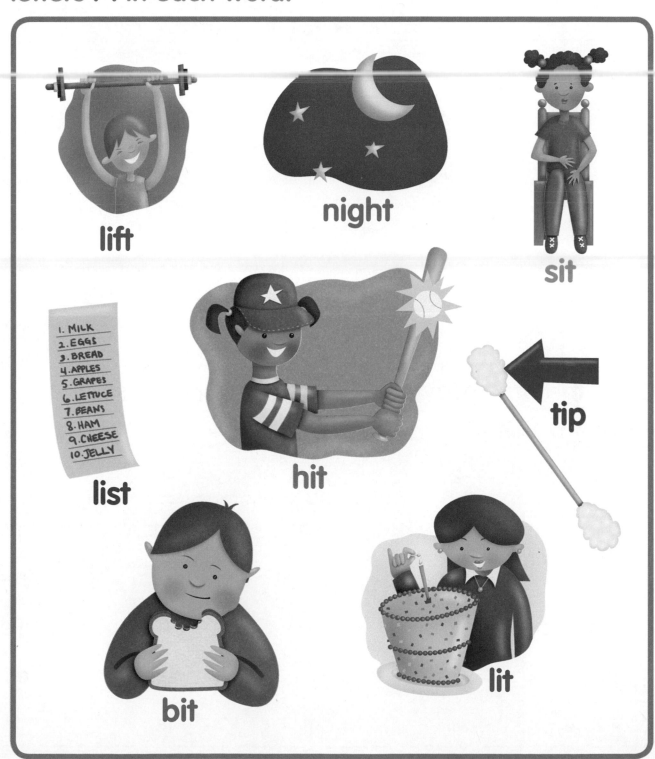

lift

night

sit

list

hit

tip

bit

lit

Review: Word Search

Find each word in the word search.

| was | three | little | help | it |

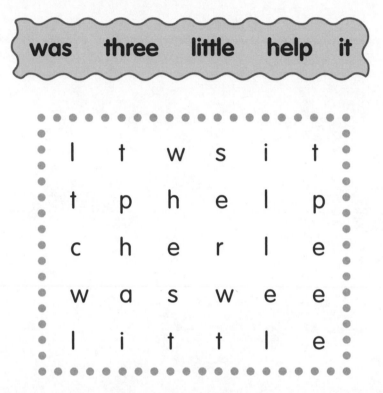

l t w s i t
t p h e l p
c h e r l e
w a s w e e
l i t t l e

Color the box that has all five review words spelled correctly.

1.	2.	3.	4.	5.
was	wos	waz	was	was
thre	three	three	threa	three
little	litlle	liltle	little	little
hlep	help	help	help	help
it	it	it	itt	it

Review: Wormy Words

Read each sentence. Every time you see one of the review words, circle it. Then count how many circled words are in each sentence.

1. It was almost three o'clock.

2. I was lost and needed a little help.

3. The cat was little, and it needed some help.

4. There were three little ducks in the pond.

5. I ate three pieces of pie.

The worm with the most words wins the race! Which worm is the winner? _____

Write your own sentence. Use as many of the review words as you can.

_____

 **no** **say the word no aloud as you trace it.**

_____

no

Now practice writing the word once on each line.

There are _____ pets allowed.

Careful Crossing

Show how the grasshopper crosses the puddle. Cross out each leaf that does not have the word **no** inside.

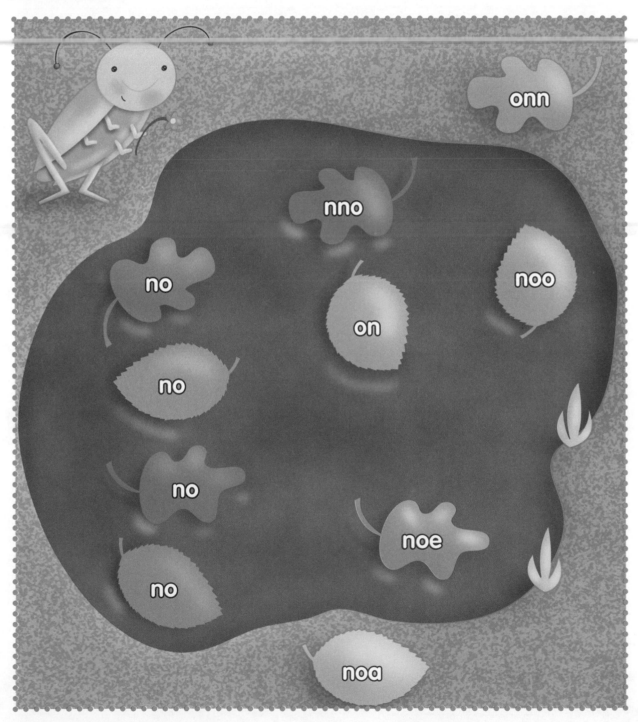

Say the word we aloud as you trace it.

Now practice writing the word once on each line.

Can _____ have ice cream?

Stay on Track

The word we is hidden two times on each track.
Find the words and circle them.

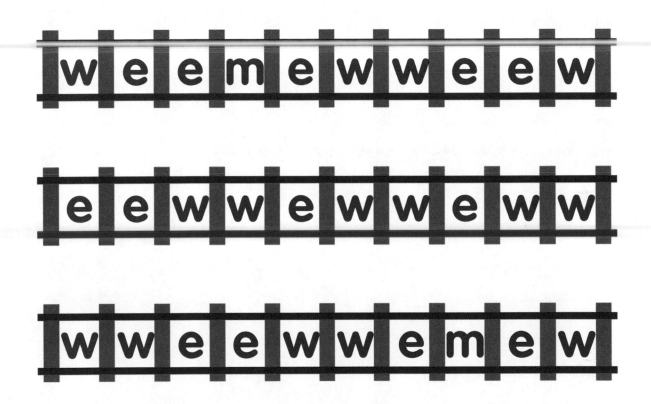

w e e m e w w e e w

e e w w e w w e w w

w w e e w w e m e w

Circle all the words that spell we.

we | we | wi | we

wee | wy | we | ew

 **say the word like aloud as you trace it.**

like

Now practice writing the word once on each line.

I _____ candy.

Lucky Letters

Write **like** on the line under each lucky clover that makes the word **like**.

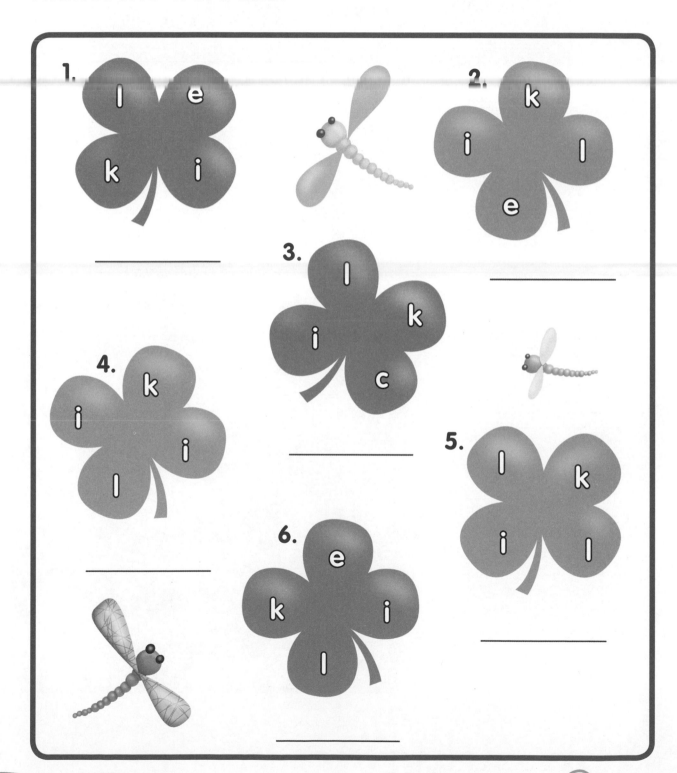

1.

l e
k i

_____

2.

k
i l
e

_____

3.

l
i k
c

_____

4.

k
i
i
l

_____

5.

l k
i l

_____

6.

e
k i
l

_____

funny say the word funny aloud as you trace it.

Now practice writing the word once on each line.

The clown is _____!

Dot-to-Dot

Draw lines to connect the letters **f-u-n-n-y** and complete the picture.

 **be**

say the word be aloud as you trace it.

be

Now practice writing the word once on each line.

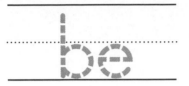

I want to _____ a fireman!

Hide and Seek

Some of the words in the treetop have **be** hidden inside. Find the words and write them on the lines below. Circle the letters **b-e** in each word.

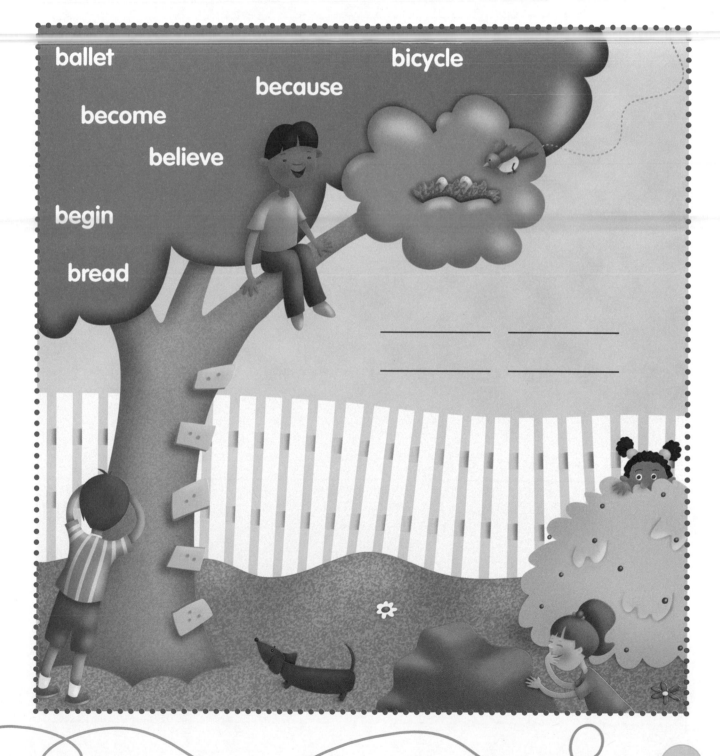

ballet

become

believe

begin

bread

because

bicycle

_____ _____

_____ _____

Review: Word Search

Find each word in the word search.

no   we   like   funny   be

```
w    l    i    k    y
f    e    s    n    i
u    y    n    a    z
n    u    o    y    b
f    l    i    k    e
```

Color the box that has all five review words spelled correctly.

1.	2.	3.	4.	5.
ro	no	mo	no	no
we	we	we	ve	we
like	like	like	licke	like
funy	funny	funni	funny	fuuny
be	be	be	be	be

Review: Wormy Words

Read each sentence. Every time you see one of the review words, circle it. Then count how many circled words are in each sentence.

1. We like to be funny! ◯

2. Can you be funny, like a clown? ◯

3. No, thank you, I don't like carrots. ◯

4. We don't like rainy days. ◯

5. We have no homework today. ◯

The worm with the most words wins the race! Which worm is the winner? _____

Write your own sentence. Use as many of the review words as you can.

_____

 **Say the word** yes **aloud as you trace it.**

_____

Now practice writing the word once on each line.

_____ , I'd like more.

Tic-Tac-Toe

Circle the row that spells the word yes.

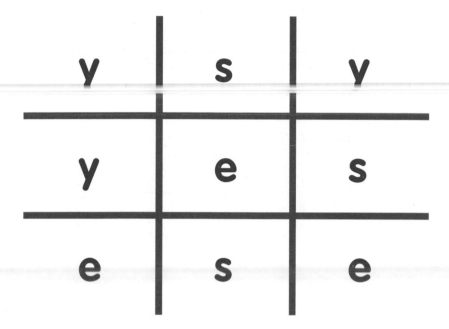

y	s	y
y	e	s
e	s	e

Circle the row that has the word yes three times.

yes	yss	yes
yee	yes	yes
yes	yes	yec

 **so** say the word **so** aloud as you trace it.

_____

⋯⋯⋯ SO ⋯⋯⋯

Now practice writing the word once on each line.

It is _____ hot.

Lost and Found

The word **so** is hidden once in each line. Find the word and circle the letters.

s	o	o	s	s	s
1	2	3	4	5	6

o	s	s	o	o	s
1	2	3	4	5	6

o	o	s	s	s	o
1	2	3	4	5	6

To complete the message, look at the number below each circled letter. Find the matching number in the message below and write the letter on the line.

Sam's ___ ___ck___ are ___n the ___t___ve.
      1 2   3   4   5 6

 **what** **Say the word what aloud as you trace it.**

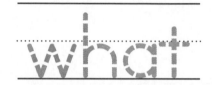

Now practice writing the word once on each line.

I wonder _____ is inside!

Linking Letters

Draw a line to link the letters that make the word what.

Write the missing letters to make the word what.

 **Say the word on aloud as you trace it.**

on

Now practice writing the word once on each line.

My books are _____ the desk.

Follow the Line

Circle the word **on** in each sentence. Then draw a line to connect the circled words, and see which letters you pass through. Write the letters below to answer the riddle.

1. It was time to put on my coat.

l   g   i   n   t

2. It wasn't hanging on the coat rack.

p   e   s   a   o

3. I looked on my bed, but no coat.

d   b   y   r   b

4. Oops! I didn't turn the lights on!

c   i   w   v   l

5. It was on the table all along.

What has four legs but can't walk?

A ___ ___ ___ ___ e!

say the word all aloud as you trace it.

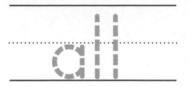

Now practice writing the word once on each line.

I used _____ the puzzle pieces.

Rhyme Time

Circle the pictures that rhyme with **all**. Underline the letters **a-l-l** in each word.

pail

call

fall

tall

salt

ball

bell

wall

Review: Word Search

Find each word in the word search.

yes   so   what   on   all

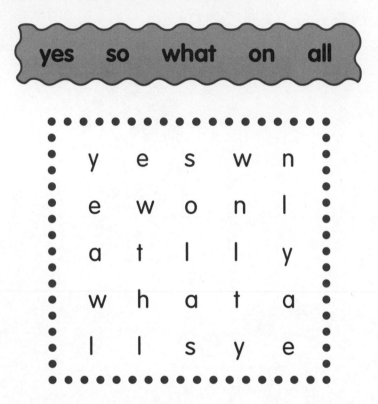

```
y  e  s  w  n
e  w  o  n  l
a  t  l  l  y
w  h  a  t  a
l  l  s  y  e
```

Color the box that has all five review words spelled correctly.

1.	2.	3.	4.	5.
yes	yas	yes	yes	yes
soo	so	so	so	so
what	what	what	what	what
on	on	onn	on	on
all	all	all	all	ali

Review: Story Surprise

Write the correct word from the word box to complete each sentence in the story.

yes   so   what   on   all

It was ___ ___ cold outside today.
      1

The ground was ___ ___ ___ covered in snow.
      2 3 4

Did we go outside? ___ ___ ___, we did!

We put ___ ___ our warm clothes.
    5 6

___ ___ ___ ___ did we do?
 7 8 9 10

For each number in the story sentences, find the matching number below. Write the letter on the line to find out what happened!

What did we do outside?
We h___d a ___ ___ ___ ___ b___ ___ ___ fig___ ___ !
     2   1 6 5 7   9 3 4   8 10

 **say the word he aloud as you trace it.**

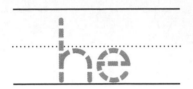

Now practice writing the word once on each line.

_____ is my brother.

Stay on Track

The word he is hidden two times on each track. Find the words and circle them.

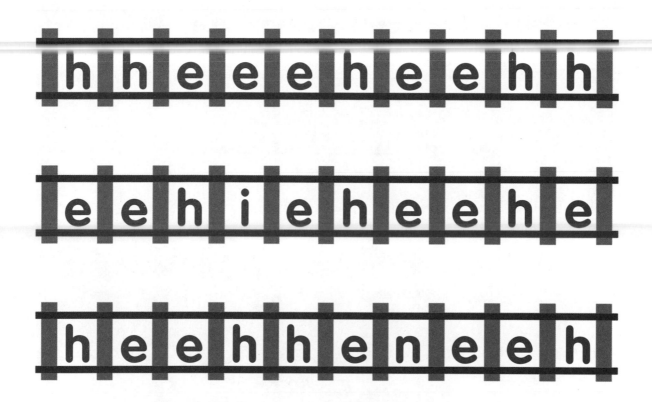

h h e e e h e e h h

e e h i e h e e h e

h e e h h h e n e e h

Circle all the words that spell he.

hi
hee
hy
he
he
hey
he
he

 **Say the word make aloud as you trace it.**

make

Now practice writing the word once on each line.

I can _____ my lunch.

Lucky Letters

Write **make** on the line under each lucky clover that makes the word **make**.

1.

2.

3.

4.

5.

6.

 **did**

say the word did aloud as you trace it.

did

Now practice writing the word once on each line.

The dog _____ it.

Tic-Tac-Toe

Circle the row that spells the word **did**.

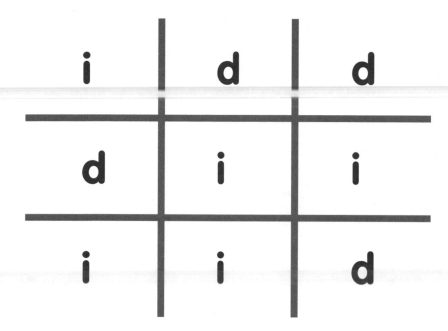

i	d	d
d	i	i
i	i	d

Circle the row that has the word **did** three times.

did	did	bid
did	did	idd
did	dib	dad

 **blue** say the word blue aloud as you trace it.

blue

Now practice writing the word once on each line.

My jeans are _____.

Lost and Found

The word blue is hidden once in each line. Find the word and circle the letters.

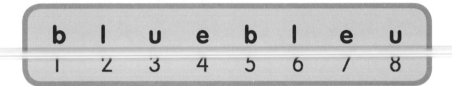

b	l	u	e	b	l	e	u
1	2	3	4	5	6	7	8

b	u	b	l	b	l	u	e
1	2	3	4	5	6	7	8

To complete the message, look at the number below each circled letter. Find the matching number in the message below and write the letter on the line.

Sam's ___as___ ___a___ ___ is ___nd___r the r___g.
       1   4   5   2   6   3   8   7

 **say the word that aloud as you trace it.**

that

Now practice writing the word once on each line.

I want _____ one.

Linking Letters

Draw a line to link the letters that make the word **that**.

Write the missing letters to make the word **that**.

Review: Word Search

Find each word in the word search.

he	make	did	blue	that

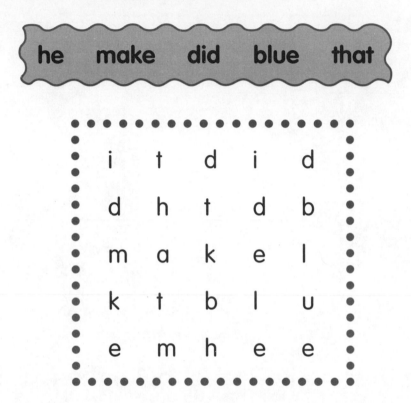

```
i  t  d  i  d
d  h  t  d  b
m  a  k  e  l
k  t  b  l  u
e  m  h  e  e
```

Color the box that has all five review words spelled correctly.

1.	2.	3.	4.	5.
he	ne	he	he	he
did	did	did	dib	did
maxe	make	make	make	make
blue	blue	blue	bloe	blue
that	that	thaf	that	that

Review: Wormy Words

Read each sentence. Every time you see one of the review words, circle it. Then count how many circled words are in each sentence.

1. He likes that blue hat. ◯

2. We can make that. ◯

3. Did he make that blue poster? ◯

4. He did all that homework. ◯

5. Did the sky look blue? ◯

The worm with the most words wins the race! Which worm is the winner? _____

Write your own sentence. Use as many of the review words as you can.

_____

Review: Puzzle

Look at each set of boxes. Find the word whose letters fit in the boxes.

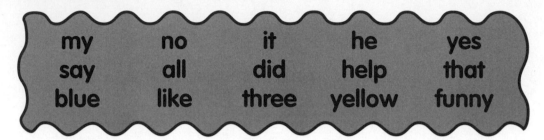

my   no   it   he   yes
say   all   did   help   that
blue   like   three   yellow   funny

1. h e

2. ☐ ☐

3. ☐ ☐

4. ☐ ☐ ☐ ☐

5. ☐ ☐ ☐ ☐ ☐

6. ☐ ☐ ☐ ☐

7. ☐ ☐ ☐

8. ☐ ☐ ☐

9. ☐ ☐ ☐

10. ☐ ☐ ☐ ☐ ☐

11. ☐ ☐ ☐

12. ☐ ☐ ☐ ☐

13. ☐ ☐ ☐ ☐ ☐ ☐

14. ☐ ☐ ☐ ☐

15. ☐ ☐

Review: Riddle

Use the code to fill in the missing letters and solve the riddle.

good: b   make: r   little: A   help: m   we: o

be: n   what: e   on: l   was: l   but: a

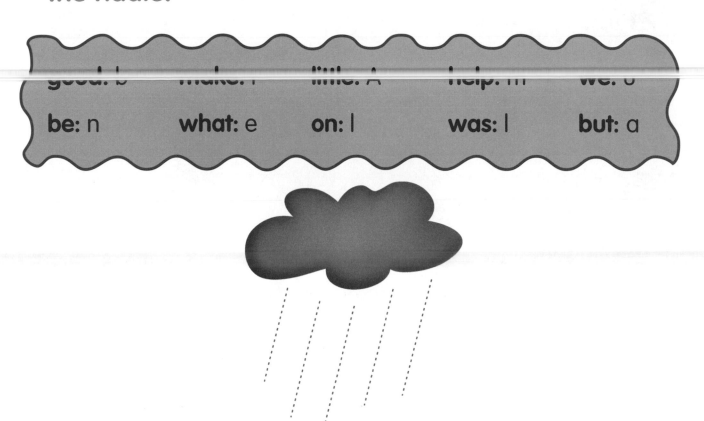

What goes up when the rain is falling down?

__ __   __ __ __ __ __ __ __ __ __

little   be   we   help   good   make   what   was   on   but

Answer Key

Page 5

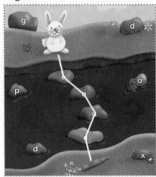

Page 7

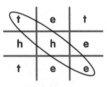

Page 9
1. up
3. up
5. up

Page 11

Page 13
These words have **for** hidden inside:
fork
form
fort
forget

Page 14

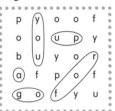

Box 2 is colored.

Page 15
1. 2
2. 3
3. 2
4. 4
5. 1
Worm 4 is the winner.
Sentences will vary.

Page 17

t	e	t
h	h	e
t	e	e

the	tbe	the
hte	teh	the
thh	the	the

Page 19

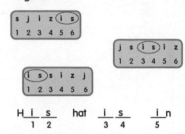

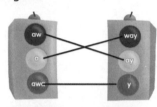

H i s hat i s i n
1 2   3 4   5

the s ink.
     6

Page 21

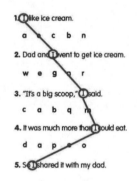

Page 23

1. I like ice cream.
   a a c b n
2. Dad and I went to get ice cream.
   w e g a r
3. "It's a big scoop," I said.
   c a b q n
4. It was much more than I could eat.
   d a p e o
5. So I shared it with my dad.

What did the cone say to the ice cream?
Dessert is o n m e!

Page 25
These pictures should be circled:
sand
stand
hand
land

Page 26

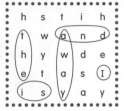

Box 4 is colored.

Page 27
My dog's name is Roofus.
I took him to the beach.
Roofus played and I swam.
Then, I couldn't find him!
Did he run away?

Where was Roofus?
Roofus was under the sand.

Page 29

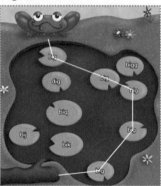

Page 31

Page 33
1. look
3. look
6. look

Page 35

Page 37
These words have **see** hidden inside:
<u>see</u>d
<u>see</u>m
<u>see</u>k
<u>see</u>saw

Page 38

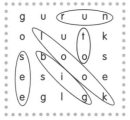

Box 1 is colored.

Page 39
1. **3**
2. **1**
3. **2**
4. **3**
5. **4**
Worm 5 is the winner.
Sentences will vary.

Page 41

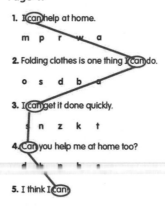

Page 43

Sa<u>m</u>'s n<u>e</u>w <u>me</u>dal is under
the <u>m</u> <u>e</u>ss.

Page 45

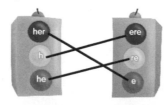

Page 47
1. I can help at home.
m p r w a
2. Folding clothes is one thing I can do.
o s d b a
3. I can get it done quickly.
s n z k t
4. Can you help me at home too?
5. I think I can!

I'm all <u>w</u> <u>a</u> <u>s</u> <u>h</u> ed up!

Page 49
These pictures should be circled:
ch<u>in</u>
p<u>in</u>
w<u>in</u>
f<u>in</u>

Page 50

Box 5 is colored.

Page 51
My brother plays hide and seek with <u>me</u>.
I can hide <u>in</u> the kitchen.
"Ready or <u>not</u>, here I come!" he says.
He'll never find me in <u>here</u>.
<u>Can</u> you find me?

Where is he?
He's hiding in the <u>cabinet</u>.

Page 53

Page 55

Page 57
2. said
4. said
5. said

Page 59

Page 61

These words have **ran** hidden inside:

<u>ran</u>ch

<u>ran</u>t

b<u>ran</u>

g<u>ran</u>d

Page 62

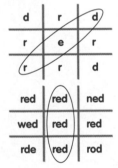

Box 3 is colored.

Page 63

1. 3
2. 4
3. 1
4. 2
5. 2

Worm 2 is the winner.
Sentences will vary.

Page 65

Page 67

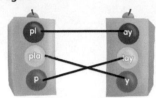

Sam's <u>d o g</u> is <u>n</u> ear the <u>w i n d o w</u>.
   1 2   4   3 8 5 6 7

Page 69

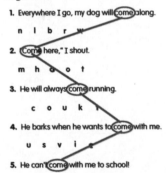

Page 71

1. Everywhere I go, my dog will (come) along.
   n l b r w
2. "(Come) here," I shout.
   m h o o t
3. He will always (come) running.
   c o u k i
4. He barks when he wants to (come) with me.
   u s v i e
5. He can't (come) with me to school!

A <u>w</u> <u>a</u> <u>t</u> <u>c</u> h dog!

Page 73

These pictures should be circled:

<u>ham</u>

c<u>lam</u>

<u>jam</u>

s<u>lam</u>

Page 74

Box 4 is colored.

Page 75

I asked Beth to <u>come</u> over.
We decided to <u>play</u> in my tree house.
Beth said, "I <u>am</u> hungry."
We didn't want to get <u>down</u> from the tree house.
What did we eat that is <u>red</u> and juicy?

What did we eat?
We ate <u>an</u> <u>apple</u> from the tree.

Page 76

2. said
3. up
4. here
5. where
6. away
7. to
8. I
9. and
10. you
11. look
12. play
13. is
14. big
15. a

Page 77

A pair of slippers

Page 79

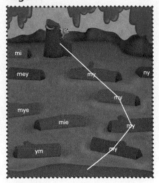

Page 81

Page 83

1. but
2. but
5. but

Page 85

Page 87

These words have **good** hidden inside:

<u>good</u>night
<u>good</u>bye
<u>good</u>ness
<u>good</u>ly

Page 88

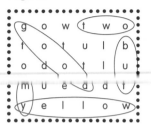

Box 1 is colored.

Page 89

There is a tree in <u>my</u> backyard.
The <u>yellow</u> lemons are ready to eat.
We had <u>two</u> yellow lemons today.
I went to pick them, <u>but</u> they were gone.
My mom used them to make something <u>good</u>!

What did she make?
A <u>glass</u> of <u>lemonade</u>.

Page 91

a	w	s
w	a	w
s	s	s

was	was	saw
mas	wsa	was
was	was	was

Page 93

Sam's s <u>h</u> <u>o</u> <u>e</u> s a <u>r</u> <u>e</u> in

t <u>he</u> <u>t</u> <u>r</u> <u>e</u> <u>e</u>.

Page 95

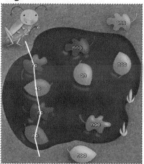

Page 97

1. I always help my mom.
   d g n u t
2. Sometimes she asks me to help make dinner.
   v s i y
3. I like to help her in the kitchen.
   t i q m
4. I can help my mom cook the food.
   u o h x
5. When dinner is ready, I can help eat it all up!

To have a well- <u>b</u> <u>a</u> <u>l</u> <u>a</u> nced meal!

Page 99

These pictures should be circled:
<u>sit</u>
<u>hit</u>
<u>lit</u>
<u>bit</u>

Page 100

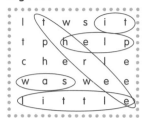

Box 5 is colored.

Page 101

1.
2. 3
3. 4
4. 2
5. 1
Worm 3 is the winner.
Sentences will vary.

Page 103

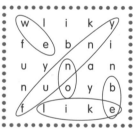

Page 105

Page 107

1. like
2. like
6. like

Page 109

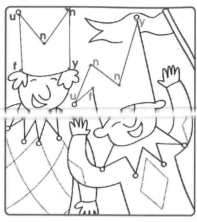

Page 111

These words have **be** hidden inside:

<u>be</u>gin
<u>be</u>come
<u>be</u>lieve
<u>be</u>cause

Page 112

Box 2 is colored.

Page 113

1. 4
2. 3
3. 2
4. 2
5. 2
Worm 1 is the winner.
Sentences will vary.

Page 115

y	s	y
y	e	s
e	s	e

(y-e-s circled across row 2)

yes	yss	yes
yee	yes	yes
yes	yes	yec

(diagonal yes circled)

Page 117

Sam's <u>s o c k s</u> are <u>o n</u>
        1 2 3 4   4

the <u>s t o v e</u>
      5   6

Page 119

Page 121

1. It was time to put on my coat.
   l g i n t

2. It wasn't hanging on the coat rack.
   p e s a o

3. I looked on my bed, but no coat.
   d b y r b

4. Oops! I didn't turn the lights on.
   c l w v l

5. It was on the table all along.
   A <u>t a b l e</u>!

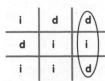

Page 123

These pictures should be circled:
c<u>all</u>
f<u>all</u>
t<u>all</u>
b<u>all</u>
w<u>all</u>

Page 124

Box 4 is colored.

Page 125

It was <u>so</u> cold outside today.
The ground was <u>all</u> covered in snow.
Did we go outside? <u>Yes</u>, we did!
We put <u>on</u> our warm clothes.
<u>What</u> did we do?

What did we do outside?
We ha<u>d</u> a <u>snowball</u> fi<u>ght</u>!

Page 127

Page 129

1. make
3. make
6. make

Page 131

i	d	d
d	i	i
i	i	d

did	did	bid
did	did	idd
did	dib	dad

Page 133

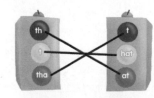

Sam's <u>b a s e b a l l</u> is
       1   4 5 2 6

<u>u</u> nd<u>e</u> r the r<u>u</u> g.
3   8   7

Page 135

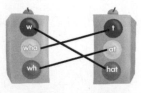

Page 136

i	t	d	i	d
d	h	t	d	b
m	a	k	e	l
k	t	b	l	u
e	m	h	e	e

Box 5 is colored.

Page 137

1. 3
2. 2
3. 5
4. 3
5. 2
Worm 3 is the winner.

Page 138

2. no
3. my
4. that
5. funny
6. help
7. all
8. did
9. say
10. three
11. yes
12. like
13. yellow
14. blue
15. it

Page 139

An umbrella